# What's the Weather?

**by Isabel Fowler**

HOUGHTON MIFFLIN    BOSTON

ISBN 10: 0-618-90006-3
ISBN 13: 978-0-618-90006-0

12 13 14 15 16 0940 21 20 19 18 17
4500648340

What is the weather where you live? Is it warm and sunny or cool and rainy? Are there four seasons, or is the weather about the same all year?

The United States has a rich variety of weather. The air in some areas is often heavy with moisture. Other areas are very dry most days. The weather may be arctic in one state and tropical in another. Mountain weather can change from sunny to stormy in minutes.

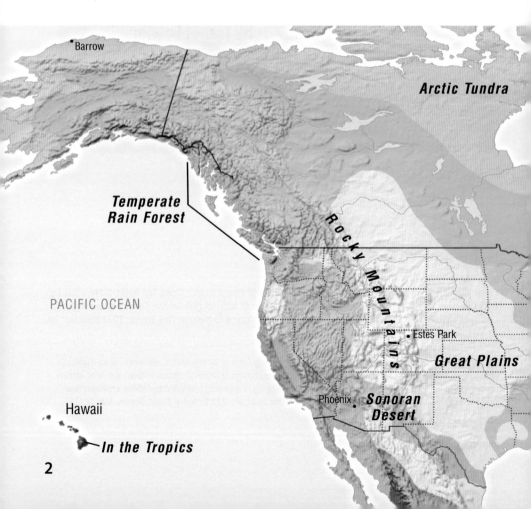

· Barrow

Arctic Tundra

Temperate
Rain Forest

Rocky Mountains

PACIFIC OCEAN

· Estes Park

Great Plains

Phoenix · Sonoran
Desert

Hawaii

In the Tropics

Why is the weather so varied? It's because of different landforms and climates. Look at the map. Can you find the temperate rain forest and desert areas? Point to the mountains, plains, tropics, and tundra shown on the map. Each area has its own climate. Do you know what the weather is in each place? Let's explore these different areas. As you read about each one, think about how its weather is special.

**Read·Think·Write** Which city on the map might often report different temperatures or moisture at noon and at 2:00 PM?

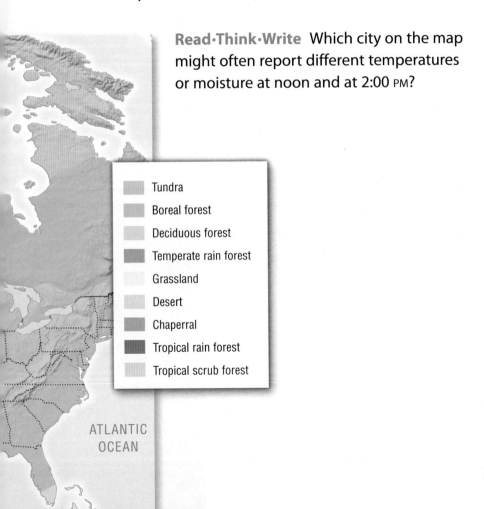

Tundra

Boreal forest

Deciduous forest

Temperate rain forest

Grassland

Desert

Chaperral

Tropical rain forest

Tropical scrub forest

ATLANTIC OCEAN

3

# Temperate Rain Forests

Many temperate rain forests are found in the Pacific Northwest. Some of these rain forests get more than 100 inches of rain per year. That's a lot of rain! Also, fog provides extra moisture for rain forest plants. Water droplets of fog cling to the parts of trees. Then the water drips onto the plants below.

What do you think the weather is in a temperate rain forest? If you guessed "mild," you are right. Winter temperatures seldom dip below 32° Fahrenheit. Summer temperatures stay around 80°F. Winters are wet and cool. Summers are foggy and mild.

**A rain forest has different layers of life.**

# Deserts

The Sonoran Desert covers part of Arizona and the southeast corner of California. Of the several deserts in the United States, the Sonoran is the hottest. It is also one of the wettest.

You probably know that most deserts get very hot during the day. Temperatures often climb above 100°F. Then at night, temperatures may drop to near freezing. Few plants grow and soak up the daytime heat. That is why temperatures tumble when the sun goes down.

Deserts do not get much moisture. In fact, most deserts get less than 10 inches of rainfall per year. When rain does fall, the water evaporates before it soaks into the ground.

**Read·Think·Write** About how many more inches of rain fall in some temperate rain forests than in most deserts?

There are cities in deserts. Phoenix, Arizona, is one of them. Because of its location, Phoenix gets very hot in the summer. Winters are pleasant, not bone chilling.

Look at the data, or recorded information, in the line graph. It shows the average high temperatures in Phoenix. More people visit this city during the winter than during the summer.

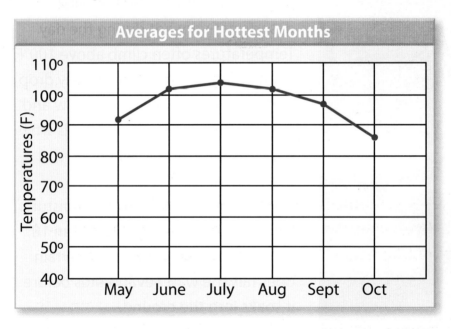

**Averages for Hottest Months**

**Read·Think·Write** Which two months have the same average temperature?

Trees cannot grow in the Arctic tundra.

## Arctic Tundra

The northernmost part of Alaska is Arctic tundra. Here, winters are long and cold. Summers are short and cool. Sometimes the tundra is called the Arctic desert. It gets about the same amount of rainfall as a desert.

The tundra is a very, very cold place. For example, the temperature in Barrow, Alaska, is below freezing during most of the year. It gets lower than 0°F much of the time.

Why is the tundra so cold? It has a layer of ground that stays frozen. That layer is called permafrost. The soil on top of permafrost may thaw, but permafrost never does. Even water cannot go through this layer.

# Mountains

The rugged Rocky Mountains stretch for about 3,000 miles. The temperature at the top of a mountain is not the same as the temperature at the bottom. The temperature drops about 3° for every 1,000 feet of height. So, if you climbed 5,000 feet (3° × 5 thousands of feet) the temperature would be 15°F colder!

**Read·Think·Write**  If the temperature is 20°F at 7,000 feet, what might the temperature be at the bottom of the mountain?

Many high mountains are snow covered.

Weather in the mountains can change quickly and without warning. In summer, thunderstorms may suddenly occur. In winter, snowstorms may happen at any time.

Days are often sunny in the Rockies. But these mountains do not get as hot as deserts can. In Estes Park, Colorado, the highest average temperature is about 78°F.

This double bar graph will help you to compare temperatures in a desert and the Rocky Mountains.

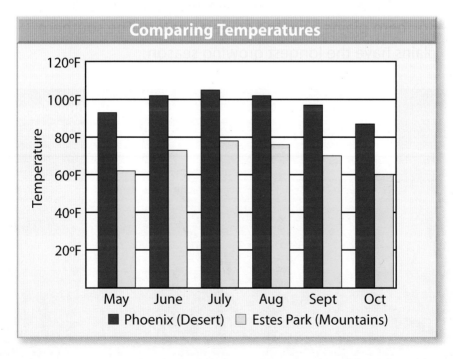

**Read·Think·Write** Which month is the hottest in both the desert and the mountains?

# The Great Plains

The Great Plains stretch across a wide area. Much of the Great Plains region has cold winters and warm summers. Strong weather is quite common. Blizzards, tornadoes, and droughts can happen.

The climate of the Great Plains differs from one area to another. The southern plains get more rain than the northern plains. There are more than twice as many warm days in the south as there are in the north. The northern plains have the coldest winters. The southern plains have the longest growing season.

The Great Plains provide much of the world's food.

# In the Tropics

The State of Hawaii is in the tropics, the warmest region of Earth. Temperatures are mild all year in the Hawaiian Islands. Average summer temperatures are in the middle eighties. Winter temperatures average about 77°F.

Some parts of the Hawaiian Islands are very dry. Others are quite wet. There is a place on the islands that gets nearly 460 inches of rain per year. As you might guess, it is the wettest place in the world! Read the data in the bar graph to compare rainfalls.

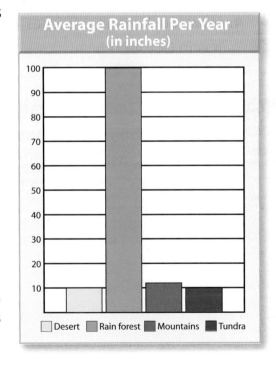

**This bar graph compares rainfall in different kinds of areas.**

**Read·Think·Write** Which areas get about the same amount of rainfall?

# Responding

**Vocabulary**

1. Look at the bar graph on page 11. Name the areas in order of their rainfalls, from least to most.

2. Look at the line graph on page 6. Do you think it will be hotter or colder in November? Why?

3. Look at the bar graph on page 9. In which months are average temperatures over 100°F in Phoenix?

4. How much warmer is Estes Park in September than it is in October?

## Activity

Determine Text Organization  List the areas you read about in this book. Then survey your classmates. Ask them which area they would most like to visit. Make a bar graph showing the results.

12